ROMANS 8:28

HE TURNS EVERYTHING FOR YOUR GOOD

MEDONA ALFRED

Made with ♥ on the Notion Press Platform
www.notionpress.com

Dedicated to my mom who is rejoicing with Jesus in heaven today.

Dedicated to my husband, who has been my great support.

Dedicated to Charlie Kirk, the late American warrior, who stood his ground for truth and proclaimed the gospel boldly unafraid of the consequences. (I was amazed to find out from his last interview with a news channel that Romans 8:28 was his favorite scripture . I believe, even though God wasn't the cause of his death, God in his magnificient wisdom has turned it for the good, where gospel reached so many more than before).

Contents

Contents

Foreword

A book backed with biblical truths, an eye opener that can change the course of your walk with the Lord.

The author has poured her heart into the book and the book is a clear evidence of her love for the body of Christ. May this revelation that God gave her to be imparted upon the next generation.

Surely this book will prune you and raise your hope in the Lord.

My confidence is that by the time you finish reading this book, the biblical truths shared here will make you free and you will be living a victorious life.

This book can be enjoyed alone or as a group study. Each chapter has enough to expound and meditate on.

So don't rush these truths. Meditate on it! Let it sink deep into your heart and my prayer for you is that you manifest Jesus. Amen!

Heartfelt blessings to all of you!

~ Sis. Priyanthy.

Preface

There is a lot of misunderstanding in the body of Christ around the will of God.

Many assume that God's will automatically comes to pass and because of which there is such a passivity the body of Christ has embraced against different tactics of the enemy.

This book aims to deal with such passivity.

But the bigger aim of the book is to reveal the "GOD of Romans 8:28" to people, that God is a master redeemer and God can turn anything evil into good for those who love Him.

Acknowledgements

I want to acknowledge first, the presence of the Holy Spirit to guide me through every page of the book, His patience to work in and through me.

Jesus, I thank you for dying in my place and forgiving my sin and send me your precious Holy Spirit.

Father, I thank you for sending your only Son for us to be our sacrifice.

I thank my husband for his love, care, support and constant encouragement.

I thank all the ministers who have played a part in this revelation taking root in me. I want to specially acknowledge Bro Andrew Wommack, Bro Col Alankamani for their contribution to the revelation in me.

I also want to acknowledge and make special mention of the book "*Eternity to Here*" by Frank Viola.

I also want to thank Purvi Menghani who helped the handwritten copy converted to a soft copy, Rushia Vats for her painting to illustrate an important point in the book, Dipika Jeswant for her help with editting.

WHAT ROMANS 8:28 DOES NOT MEAN!

CHAPTER ONE

INTRODUCING YOU TO ROMANS 8:28

Romans 8:28

"And we know that all things work together for good to those who love God, to those who are the called according to His purpose."

In my opinion, this is one of the most misinterpreted passage of scriptures in the body of Christ.

Reading this scripture, people come to an understanding that everything happening in their life is God-sent and everything- the good, bad and ugly is from God . Most people automatically assume that it is good because they believe God sent it in their life.

We tend to understand it this way because of the messages or sermons we have heard and we have read it into this scripture.

What does this scripture actually say? It doesn't say "Everything that happens is of God and is good". It says "ALL THINGS WORK TOGETHER FOR GOOD TO THOSE

WHO LOVE GOD".

I want to turn your attention to the words, "ALL THINGS WORK TOGETHER FOR GOOD" and to the qualifier mentioned, "THOSE WHO LOVE GOD".

It is important to understand that not everything that is happening in the world is of God. For Example, COVID is not of God, it is of the devil. How do we know? John 10:10 says,

> "*The thief does not come except to steal, and to kill, and to destroy. I have come that they may have life, and that they may have it more abundantly.*"

So, not everything that happens is automatically God's will. There is an enemy called the devil who is fiercely on the move to kill, steal and destroy.

CHAPTER TWO

THE RIGHT OWNER

Let's look into this passage of scripture:

"*Matthew 12:22-32*

*Then one was brought to Him who was demon-possessed, blind and mute; and He healed him, so that the blind and mute man both spoke and saw. And all the multitudes were amazed and said, "Could this be the Son of David?" Now when the Pharisees heard it they said, "**This fellow does not cast out demons except by Beelzebub, the ruler of the demons**." But Jesus knew their thoughts, and said to them: "Every kingdom divided against itself is brought to desolation, and every city or house divided against itself will not stand. If Satan casts out Satan, he is divided against himself. How then will his kingdom stand? And if I cast out demons by Beelzebub, by whom do your sons cast them out? Therefore they shall be your judges. But if I cast out demons by the Spirit of God, surely the kingdom of God has come upon you. Or how can one enter a* *strong man's house and plunder his goods, unless he first binds the strong man? And then he will plunder his house. He who is not with Me is against Me, and he who does not gather with Me scatters abroad. **"Therefore I say to you, every sin and blasphemy will be forgiven men, but the blasphemy against the Spirit will not be forgiven men.** Anyone who speaks a word against the Son of Man, it will be forgiven him; but whoever speaks against the Holy Spirit, it will not be forgiven him, either in this age or in the age to come."*

People accused Jesus of casting demons out by the power of Beelzebub when it was actually by the power of the Holy Spirit that He cast them out. Jesus detests it and calls it a sin.

Here, the Pharisees call what is of God as something as of the devil. On the other hand, today, there are some who call what is of the devil as something that is of God.

Calling what is of God as of the devil and what is of the devil is as of God are equally erroneous, or more appropriately dangerous.

The above incident gives an invitation, or more so, a strong instruction to attribute the works to the rightful source or rightful owner and also to not attribute the works to the wrong owner.

So understanding the right owner and right source becomes a no-option quest for us as believers before we pronounce a judgement over any kind of work.

CHAPTER THREE

WILL THE WILL OF GOD AUTOMATICALLY COME TO PASS?

No. The will of God does not come to pass automatically.

People assume that God's will in their life will automatically come to pass. No, it has to be pursued and before it is pursued, it has to be understood.

If the will of God automatically comes to pass on earth, then Jesus wouldn't have needed to pray "Let your will be done on earth as it is in heaven".

"Your kingdom come, your will be done, on earth as it is in heaven." (Matthew 6:10)

If it was prayed for, it directly implies that it is yet to happen. No one prays for something that has already happened.

In heaven, the will of God is on the full swing. But Jesus who is from the bosom of the Father sees and knows that God's will is not being done on earth entirely, the way it is in heaven. This is very reason He prays the above prayer.

Let's look into few more scriptures:

2 Peter 3:9

"The Lord is not slack concerning His promise, as some count slackness, but is longsuffering toward us, not willing that any should perish but that all should come to repentance."

1 Timothy 2:4

"...who desires all men to be saved and to come to the knowledge of the truth."

According to this verse, is it God's will that no one should perish? Yes.

Is it God's will that all men be saved? Yes.

But is it happening? No.

Even though God wants all men be saved and come to the knowledge of truth, God needs man to agree with Him in his heart and confess with his mouth that Jesus Christ is Lord, for him to be saved (Romans 10:9).

What does that tell us? God can have a will for someone but that person can live outside His (God's) will through his own will. In other words, you and I have a part to play in His will coming to pass in our lives.

Many have a big challenge in coming to terms with that truth. The first question that arises after this truth is shared is "God knows everything. How can you say that God didn't cause that to happen. Isn't that undermining God's power to foresee things?". It is a great question. I struggled with this for a long time.

But this question stems from a place of not understanding the difference between foreknowledge and control. God can foresee things. He sees the end from the beginning. 100% true. But that does not mean He controls the outcome.

For example, "Did God cause Adam to sin?" Any one of us would say "No!". If everything that happens is controlled by God, wouldn't it be right to say, 'God caused Adam to sin'? Yet, we know God did not cause Adam to sin but Adam chose to sin because of his freewill.

So if God foreknew Adam would sin, why didn't He stop him or control him?

Can you imagine, God used His foreknowledge to make Jesus the lamb slain before the foundations of the world but He didn't use His foreknowledge to control Adam. Wow! There is a revelation right there!

God is love. Out of His Love, out of His nature He gave man something called "free will". God is someone refuses to take back whatever He has given freely, regardless of the outcome. That is God, that is His nature!

That is our God!

God doesn't use His foreknowledge to control man but He used His foreknowledge to "control" His response. If He uses it to control man, that isn't Love. Love doesn't force, Love doesn't control. If He does, He would contradict His very nature, He would contradict Himself, which He wouldn't, in a million years.

So, in conclusion, we understand that God has foreknowledge of all things but inspite of His foreknowledge he does not control man's choices and therefore does not control the outcome.

CHAPTER FOUR

THANK GOD IN EVERYTHING

1 Thesalonians 5:16-18 NKJV

"[16] Rejoice always,

[17] pray without ceasing,

[18] in everything give thanks; for this is the will of God in Christ Jesus for you."

Many people try to apply this verse and thank God for everything that happens.

Let me give you an example. Say I visit your house and you tell me "Hey thank you for your gift yesterday", you implicitly mean that I gave you the gift and you are thankful for it.

In the same way, when you give thanks for all your problems—especially the ones you are facing right now that do not line up with the Word of God—you are indirectly saying that He caused the problem or allowed it in your life.

That is why we cannot thank God for every situation, because He is not the one who orchestrates all of them. But we can thank Him in every situation, regardless of the circumstance, because even in the midst of something undesirable, there are always genuine reasons to give thanks to God.

For example, may be someone met with an accident. It isn't appropriate for us to thank God for the accident, because God didn't cause it or allow it. But we can definitely thank God that the Lord protected him without injuries, for His promise of angels over him protecting him in the midst of such situations.

So we cannot thank God for everything but surely we can and should thank Him in everything.

CHAPTER FIVE

CALL IT WHAT IT IS!

Many people fail to recognise the difference between a blessing and a curse.

Some people embrace certain curses as a "blessing in disguise".

No, a blessing is a blessing and a curse is a curse. We need to learn to call it what it is, for us to be able to deal with it the right way.

If a doctor detects a cancer in someone's body and suggests that the tumour was present to nourish his body, the doctor is going to let that cancer kill that person.

The same way, if we somehow embrace 'curses' as blessings from God, we wouldn't be built to resist it, neither in our thoughts nor in our lives.

Let me just list down certain blessings and curses for you so that you understand what a blessing is and what is not.

The set of blessings:
Deutronomy 28:1-14
[1] "Now it shall come to pass, if you diligently obey the voice of the Lord your God, to observe carefully all

His commandments which I command you today, that the Lord your God will set you high above all nations of the earth. [2] And all these blessings shall come upon you and overtake you, because you obey the voice of the Lord your God: [3] "Blessed shall you be in the city, and blessed shall you be in the country. [4] "Blessed shall be the fruit of your body, the produce of your ground and the increase of your herds, the increase of your cattle and the offspring of your flocks. [5] "Blessed shall be your basket and your kneading bowl. [6] "Blessed shall you be when you come in, and blessed shall you be when you go out. [7] "The Lord will cause your enemies who rise against you to be defeated before your face; they shall come out against you one way and flee before you seven ways. [8] "The Lord will command the blessing on you in your storehouses and in all to which you set your hand, and He will bless you in the land which the Lord your God is giving you. [9] "The Lord will establish you as a holy people to Himself, just as He has sworn to you, if you keep the commandments of the Lord your God and walk in His ways. [10] Then all peoples of the earth shall see that you are called by the name of the Lord, and they shall be afraid of you. [11] And the Lord will grant you plenty of goods, in the fruit of your body, in the increase of your livestock, and in the produce of your ground, in the land of which the Lord swore to your fathers to give you. [12] The Lord will open to you His good treasure, the heavens, to give the rain to your land in its season, and to bless all the work of your hand. You shall lend to many nations, but you shall not borrow. [13] And the Lord will make you the head and not the tail; you shall be above only, and not be beneath, if you heed the commandments of the Lord your God, which I command you today, and are careful to observe them. [14]

So you shall not turn aside from any of the words which I command you this day, to the right or the left, to go after other gods to serve them.

The set of curses:

Deutronomy 28:15-57

[15] But it shall come to pass, if you do not obey the voice of the Lord your God, to observe carefully all His commandments and His statutes which I command you today, that all these curses will come upon you and overtake you: [16] "Cursed shall you be in the city, and cursed shall you be in the country. [17] "Cuersed shall be your basket and your kneading bowl. [18] "Cursed shall be the fruit of your body and the profduce of your land, the increase of your cattle and the offspring of your flocks. [19] "Cursed shall you be when you come in, and cursed shall you be when you go out. [20] "The Lord will send on you cursing, confusion, and rebuke in all that you set your hand to do, until you are destroyed and until you perish quickly, because of the wickedness of your doings in which you have forsaken Me. [21] The Lord will make the plague cling to you until He has consumed you from the land which you are going to possess. [22] The Lord will strike you with consumption, with fever, with inflammation, with severe burning fever, with the sword, with scorching, and with mildew; they shall pursue you until you perish. [23] And your heavens which are over your head shall be bronze, and the earth which is under you shall be iron. [24] The Lord will change the rain of your land to powder and dust; from the heaven it shall come down on you until you are destroyed. [25] "The Lord will cause you to be defeated before your enemies; you shall go out one way against them and flee seven ways before them; and you shall become troublesome to all the kingdoms of the earth. [26] Your

carcasses shall be food for all the birds of the air and the beasts of the earth, and no one shall frighten them away. [27] The Lord will strike you with the boils of Egypt, with tumors, with the scab, and with the itch, from which you cannot be healed. [28] The Lord will strike you with madness and blindness and confusion of heart. [29] And you shall grope at noonday, as a blind man gropes in darkness; you shall not prosper in your ways; you shall be only oppressed and plundered continually, and no one shall save you. [30] "You shall betroth a wife, but another man shall lie with her; you shall build a house, but you shall not dwell in it; you shall plant a vineyard, but shall not gather its grapes. [31] Your ox shall be slaughtered before your eyes, but you shall not eat of it; your donkey shall be violently taken away from before you, and shall not be restored to you; your sheep shall be given to your enemies, and you shall have no one to rescue them. [32] Your sons and your daughters shall be given to another people, and your eyes shall look and fail with longing for them all day long; and there shall be no strength in your hand. [33] A nation whom you have not known shall eat the fruit of your land and the produce of your labor, and you shall be only oppressed and crushed continually. [34] So you shall be driven mad because of the sight which your eyes see. [35] The Lord will strike you in the knees and on the legs with severe boils which cannot be healed, and from the sole of your foot to the top of your head. [36] "The Lord will bring you and the king whom you set over you to a nation which neither you nor your fathers have known, and there you shall serve other gods—wood and stone. [37] And you shall become an astonishment, a proverb, and a byword among all nations where the Lord will drive you. [38] "You shall carry much seed out to the field but gather little in, for the locust shall consume it. [39] You shall plant vineyards and tend them, but you shall neither drink of the wine nor gather the grapes; for the worms shall eat them. [40] You shall have olive trees throughout all your territory, but you shall not anoint yourself with the oil; for your olives shall drop off. [41] You shall beget sons and daughters, but they shall not be yours; for they shall go into captivity. [42] Locusts shall consume all your trees and the produce of your land. [43] "The alien who is among you shall rise higher and higher above you, and you shall come down lower and lower. [44] He shall lend to you, but you shall not lend to him; he shall be the head, and you shall be the tail. [45] "Moreover all these curses shall come upon you and pursue and overtake you, until you are destroyed, because you did not obey the voice of the Lord your God, to keep His commandments and His statutes which He commanded you. [46] And they shall be upon you for a sign and a wonder, and on your descendants forever. [47] "Because you did not serve the Lord your God with joy and gladness of heart, for the abundance of everything, [48] therefore you shall serve your enemies, whom the Lord will send against you, in hunger, in thirst, in nakedness, and in need of everything; and He will put a yoke of iron on your neck until He has destroyed you. [49] The Lord will bring a nation against you from afar, from the end of the earth, as swift as the eagle flies, a nation whose language you will not understand, [50] a nation of fierce countenance, which does not respect the elderly nor show favor to the young. [51] And they shall eat the increase of your livestock and the produce of your land, until you are destroyed; they shall not leave you grain or new wine or oil, or the increase of your cattle or the offspring of your flocks, until they have destroyed you. [52] "They shall besiege you at all your gates until your high and fortified walls, in which you trust, come down throughout all your land; and they shall besiege you at all your gates throughout all your land which the Lord your God has given you. [53] You shall eat the fruit of your own body, the flesh of your sons and your daughters whom the Lord your God has given you, in the siege and desperate straits in which your enemy shall distress you. [54] The sensitive and very refined man among you will be hostile toward his brother, toward the wife of his bosom, and toward the rest of his children whom he leaves behind, [55] so that he will not give any of them the flesh of his children whom he will eat, because he has nothing left in the siege and desperate straits in which your enemy shall distress you at all your gates. [56] The tender and delicate woman among you, who would not venture to set the sole of her foot on the ground because of her delicateness and sensitivity, will refuse to the husband of her bosom, and to her son and her daughter, [57] her placenta which comes out from between her feet and her children whom she bears; for she will eat them secretly for lack of everything in the siege and desperate straits in which your enemy shall distress you at all your gates.

Deuteronomy 28 – Blessings vs Curses

	Blessings (v.1–14)	Curses (v.15–68)
City & Country	Blessed in the city and in the field.	Cursed in the city and in the field:
Family / Children	Blessed offspring; increase in family and livestock.	Children afflicted; loss of children; family broken.
Work & Produce	Blessed basket and kneading bowl; crops	Cursed basket and kneading bowl; crops fail.
Health	God gives health and protection.	Disease; plagues, boils, sickness, blindness.
Protection from Enemies	Enemies defeated; they flee in seven ways.	Enemies defeat you; you flee in seven ways; oppression.
Weather / Land	Rain in season: land produces abundantly	Drought, bronze sky, iron ground; blight and mildew.
Success / Defeat	Head and not tail; move upward only.	Tail and not head; always downward.
Prosperity	Abundant goods; full storehouses; God blesses all you do.	Poverty, hunger, thirst; nakedness; borrowing, not lending.
Relationships with Nations	You lend to many nations; do not borrow.	You borrow and serve enemies; foreigners rise above you.
Joy / Fear	Joyful life under God's favor.	Constant fear, sorrow, hopelessness.

Blessing vs Curses

Let's take an example from here. Here we clearly see that sickness/disease is listed down here as a curse and not a blessing.

A sickness is never a 'blessing in disguise'. A sickness isn't sent by God to teach you anything. It came from the devil to destroy you. Holy Spirit was the person sent by God to teach you. He doesn't need the aid of sickness if He wants to teach you something. That's belittling the teaching capacity of the Holy Spirit.

A Blessing Definition: (in my understanding)

It is the power of God unleashed in your life to prosper you in every area of your life, inside out and empower you to walk and possess everything God has created you for.

Curse Definition: (in my understanding)

It's a power unleashed to rob you of every good thing God created you for and destroy your life and future.

Galatians 3:13 says "Christ has redeemed us from the curse of the law, having become a curse for us (for it is written, "Cursed is everyone who hangs on a tree"),

This scripture says Christ became a curse for us so that we don't have to experience any curse. If you are experiencing any kind of curse, or curses mentioned above, it is against the will of God for your life. If you are experiencing any of it now, it has to be cursed and cast away and not to be embraced and retained as a blessing.

CHAPTER SIX

SICK FOR GOD'S GLORY?

In my opinion, the following passages are among the highly misunderstood scripture passages in the bible.

John 9:1-3

'Now as Jesus passed by, He saw a man who was blind from birth. And His disciples asked Him, saying, "Rabbi, who sinned, this man or his parents, that he was born blind?" Jesus answered, "Neither this man nor his parents sinned, but that the works of God should be revealed in him.'

And,

John 11:4.

'When Jesus heard that, He said, "This sickness is not unto death, but for the glory of God, that the Son of God may be glorified through it."'

I hear your question. Isn't Jesus saying that the blind man was blind so that the works of God should be revealed in him? So doesn't that mean God made him blind so that He could reveal Himself in him?

So let's consider a human parallel and let's see how that plays out.

There was this man who was often misunderstood by the people around him.

He somehow wanted to show his people that he wasn't evil but good. So one day, he made a plan. He decided to bruise his child in the bedroom and let him go in the public-crying, yelling in pain.

And when the child was bleeding, crying out in pain, he immediately runs to him with medicines trying to clean and dress his wounds, applying ointment etc.

What would we call this man now? Is this love or selfishness? What would you comment on this man's character?

If you judge right, you could see that this man was selfish, actually-cruel. Then how do you expect your perfect heavenly Father to embody such a character trait?

Matthew 7:11

"If you then, being evil, know how to give good gifts to your children, how much more will your Father who is in heaven give good things to those who ask Him!"

Your heavenly Father is always so much greater and overflowing with Love and goodness than any earthly father.

Look this scripture:

Acts 10:38

"how God anointed Jesus of Nazareth with the Holy Spirit and with power, who went about doing good and healing all who were oppressed by the devil, for God was with Him."

By whom were the people oppressed? God? No, the devil. Sickness is an oppression of the devil.

And God's word records healing to be 'good'. God anointed Jesus to heal and God declares healing to be 'good'. He didn't approve sickness or oppression to be 'good', rather He affirms the freedom from it to be 'good'.

God's not the source of evil in this world. Jesus came to destroy the evil works of the devil on this earth.

I think, we have established enough on what this scripture (John 9:1-3) does not say. Now we'll have to get to the part of what it actually says.

But wait, what about Lazarus? Jesus said, he died for His glory. So wasn't this death for Jesus' glory?

No, it was not. If it was, Jesus wouldn't say that "this sickness is not unto death".

If you have to really understand the heart of God, you need to look back at Eden or you need to look at how heaven is and how it functions.

Was there death in Eden? No.

Was there sickness in Eden? No!

Is there death or sickness in heaven? No.

These are places where God's perfect will is on force and you don't find death or sickness here.

Then what makes us think He acts different here with us?

God was not the one who made him blind or caused Lazarus to die nor did he allow it.

'Then what did He actually mean"' is a question that still stands.

When the Lord was teaching me on divine healing, these were the main passages that stood in the way of everything I believed in, until God directly taught me one day what these scriptures actually meant.

One day, I was out for a hospital to pray for the sick. I used to often go to hospitals to pray and get the sick healed and this was one such instance.

As I moved from bed to bed, praying for them, I came to this particular person and asked her what her problem was.

I think she had mentioned stomach pain. I immediately jumped and said, "Wow! That's awesome".

She looked at me puzzled for a minute. Then I commanded the pain to leave and it left. She became completely free.

After this incident, the Lord started speaking to me. He asked me, "Why were you excited when she shared about her pain? Was it because she was in pain?"

I said "No, Lord". It's because 'I knew that the pain will leave in another few minutes. It's because I had already seen in my heart what was going to happen."

Then the Lord taught me these passages. I instantly knew in me what these passages of scripture meant.

The Lord is always victorious. He doesn't know what it is to be defeated. He has never been defeated all His life and He never will be.

He only knows victory and sees victory. In any given situation, He can only see victory because he is the 'I AM' and He knows who He is.

FATE/DESTINY OF ANY GIVEN 'SITUATION' IS NOT DEPENDENT ON HOW THE SITUATION LOOKS LIKE
BUT BY WHO HE IS.

For eg, Naman can be a leaper, it can look like Naaman will die in leprosy. But because He is the Jehovah Rapha he will not remain a leaper, and he didn't remain a leper.

A situation's destiny is not dependent of what it is but is solely dependent on WHO HE IS.

When God saw Abram and Sarai, He saw Abraham as the Father of many nations and Sarah-mother of many nations because of who He is. And He spoke what He wanted to see not what the natural situation looks like.

His power and His nature decides how anyone or any situation will come to look like.

The same way, when the Lord saw the blind man, he was already seeing the power of God manifest in Him. He wouldn't exalt the problem or his situation or the demons who caused the situation by speaking about it. But He would speak only the end result.

Let me put it this way. Have you ever seen movies where there is a hero and a villain. I don't know about other languages but most Tamil movies have such kind of dialogues by the heroes towards the Villain.

"Hey! Do you know why you are here? You are here just to die in my hands". There is an attitude behind it: an ever-winning attitude.

The glory was through the healing, not through the sickness. We never bring glory to God through our sickness.

Which of the sick soldiers have brought glory to the army through their sickness? It is his health which is the glory of the army. So it is, with the Kingdom of God.

That's the same attitude with which Jesus speaks this. He says, 'this sickness is here just to get destroyed in my hands'. 'This death happened just so that would have glory.'

Glory to Jesus, the ever victorious lamb of God and the Savior of the world.

CHAPTER SEVEN

THE EXPECTED END

If only what God has decided is going to come to pass in your life and you have no say in it, then why do you pray? Why should anyone pray, read the bible, seek God?

If God says pray, does it not imply that our asking, believing and seeking has an effect on what we experience?

Yes, God is God and nobody teaches him anything or instructs Him anything.

> "*Jeramiah 29:11*
>
> *For I know the thoughts that I think toward you, says the Lord, thoughts of peace and not of evil, to give you a future and a hope.*"

But His thoughts towards you are peace already. The scripture continues to say, His thoughts are to give you an expected end. If God's will is mysterious like most people think, how could God give you an EXPECTED end.

The fact that you can expect it, implies that it isn't mysterious anymore. God has revealed it to us through His Word and His Spirit.

Many people think they can never understand God, His will and His thoughts. They often quote this scripture:

> "*1 Corinthians 2:9 (NKJV)*
> *But as it is written:*
> *"Eye has not seen, nor ear heard,*
> *<u>Nor have entered into the heart of man</u>*
> *The things which God has prepared for those who love Him."*"

People think the things of God is so mysterious and it can never into the heart of man.

But let context decide its interpretation:

The very next scripture says

> "*1 Corinthians 2:10 (NKJV)*
> *But God has revealed them to us through His Spirit. For the Spirit searches all things, yes, the deep things of God.*"

We have the great privilege of recieving the indwelling presence of the Holy Spirit and the above scripture says "God has revealed it to us through His Spirit". We have access to knowing His will now through His Word and His Spirit.

I am reminded of a minister of God who once shared this incident. He was trying to explain to someone that we have a part to play in experiencing God's will in our lives. This person kept arguing, kept resisting and at last this minister slapped this person. When the person became furious, he said, 'You can't slap me back or hurt me because you didn't get slapped without it being the will of God, as you have always believed.'

I am not sure if that man got the point. But I certainly did.

GOD'S WILL DOES NOT COME TO PASS AUTOMATICALLY.

IT HAS TO BE PURSUED, UNDERSTOOD AND BELIEVED.

CHAPTER EIGHT

KNOWING IS THE BRIDGE

KNOWING IS KEY, KNOWING IS THE BRIDGE

So then how does the will of God come to pass in my life? How do I pursue the will of God? How do I experience His will in my life. Simple!

The first step or I would say the only step to experience His will is your life is KNOW THE WILL.

> "*Hosea 4:6*
>
> *My people are destroyed for lack of knowledge.*
> *Because you have rejected knowledge,*
> *I also will reject you from being priest for Me;*
> *Because you have forgotten the law of your God,*
> *I also will forget your children.*"

"My people perish because of lack of knowledge"

This knowledge He mentions is not general knowledge. He is talking about the knowledge of God.

Let's look into one more important passage of scripture.

> "*John 17:3*

"And this is eternal life, that they may know You, the only true God, and Jesus Christ whom You have sent.""

"Knowing God is Eternal Life".

The word "know" here could derive it's fuller sense if we look into the scripture in Genesis 4:1

"Now Adam knew Eve his wife, and she conceived and bore Cain, and said, "I have acquired a man from the Lord.""

The *knowing* John 17:3 talks about isn't an intellectual knowing but an experiencial knowing like the knowing of Genesis 4:1. Adam knowing his wife wasn't an intellectual knowing, it was an intimate knowing. When we *know* God intimately, that is when we experience His Word and His will in our lives.

Every moment of knowing Him sparks and releases eternal life into experience in our lives.

You experience His life only when you know Him.

You come under the reign of His will, when you come to the understanding of His will.

But can you really know God's will?

"Ephesians 5:17

Therefore do not be unwise, but understand what the will of the Lord is."

If we had no access to understanding God's will, we wouldn't have this scripture in the Bible. The Spirit of God in us empowers us to understand the will of God.

God's Word is God's will. If the Word of God promises a child of God something, we can rest assured that it is God's will for us.

We experience His will consistently when we know His will. For example, God has promised me divine health in the scriptures around two thousand years ago. But first sixteen years of my life, I struggled with frequent sickness because I didn't know His will for my life with regard to physical health. But when I did understand the truth when I was around sixteen,that I was healed by His stripes, immediately it started affecting my health God's way. It is almost 15 years since I have visited a doctor for myself. God healed me of multiple problems.

> "*1 Peter 2:24....*
> *by whose stripes you were healed.*"

God didn't suddenly change His mind when I was sixteen. It was all along God's will. But I understood His will only when I was sixteen. And understanding His will regarding my health changed everything for me.

Hence, if we expect to experience God's will in our lives, it is crucial that we seek to understand His Will from His Word and through His Spirit.

Knowing is the bridge between the 'will of God that is available' to the 'will of God that we experience'.

Bridge that connects two important structures

MY PERSONAL EXPERIENCE

CHAPTER NINE

MY PERSONAL ENCOUNTER

The Lord has been speaking of 'Romans 8:28' to me for the past 5 years now that this is the time the body of Christ is going to greatly experience this scripture.

It is Romans 8:28 days for the body of Christ!

Because of the predominant traditions and opinions of man around this scripture I have dedicated this first 6 chapters just to deal with the traditions and explaining what Romans 8:28 'does not say' because the traditions make the Word of God of no effect.

"Mark 7:13

making the word of God of no effect through your tradition"

It is from this part of the book that I am going to be explaining what 'Romans 8:28 does say'.

I am going to begin with sharing my own personal experience.

I was in a meeting and there was someone preaching on the pulpit . At the same time, my spiritual eyes opened and

I began to see an open vision. The preaching had nothing to do with it but I saw something strange, something I had never seen before.

I saw myself on a stage standing on the pulpit with a microphone and I saw there were so many sick people — but it was just ugly sickness. People were deformed, people were with diseases that totally changed their appearance into an ugly appearance. I understood in myself without any words, that it was the demons trying to intimidate me, saying 'look what I have done to these people'. It was an effort to intimidate me saying that those sicknesses were greater than I could handle.

And I remember that I was on the pulpit and I just started laughing and laughing and laughing, uncontrollably laughing. And I instinctively felt that the demons were wondering why I was laughing. As I was laughing, the Lord because of His super abounding wisdom started releasing prophetic messages from that place, from those very same weaknesses/sicknessess. And as I released or made use of those prophetic messages, these sicknesses were fleeing out of that place and people were being made free.

In other words, in the midst of all the chaos the demons brought in, the Lord generated messages out of them, made those very same weaknesses serve Him and His kingdom, And as I preached/delivered that message, those ugly demons were fleeing that place.

I didn't understand much of that vision, I didn't know it had so much to do with my life from that day forward.

After that vision that Lord made this scripture come so alive to me.

"*Romans 8:28*

"And we know that all things work together for good to those who love God, to those who are the called according to His purpose."
"

He strategically placed this scripture around me every place I saw. I saw it in the most unlikely places I could ever see it. I knew He was trying to get my attention and tell me something.

CHAPTER TEN

AN EXPERIENCE THAT EXPLAINS

When such supernatural experiences and downloads occur, one instinctively and instantly understands so many things which might need hours of explanation to communicate.

In this vision I instantly knew certain things which I don't think I could fully convey while narrating the vision in the previous chapter.

I am inspired to share this incident with you which might serve as an explanatory story covering up for what I couldn't convey in the previous chapter(narration).

Once we were ministering as a team in a church. Among us was a brother in the Lord, who moves very sharp in the prophetic, specially with words of knowledge.

It so happened that when we were worshiping, this man was so taken by the presence of God that his entire body was shaking and shivering.

He asked for a small piece of paper and he started writing something in it. I happened to be near the place where people were registering themselves with their names and numbers.

He sent that piece of paper and sent word to the registration desk to check if there was anyone who has registered with that phone number.

I went to check and was surprised to see a phone number exactly identical to what he had written in that paper except for the difference in the last number.

He had written '9854231259' [random number,for example] instead of '9854231256'. Still I was in awe and told myself 'Maybe he missed 1 number when hearing from God'.

The Shivering numbers

During the meeting, this brother said that the Lord wanted him to call this sister. When he called her out and asked if the number he mentioned was her phone number, she replied, "I'm not sure of my phone number; I have a small diary where I've written it down."

And there she pulled out her old small torn-up diary and turned to the page where she had written her phone number. As I looked into it, I was filled with awe.

I discovered that the number she had written in the registration desk was wrong . What this prophet had written in his small little paper with his shivering hands was right.

It took a while for me to recover from the awe I was filled with. From this one incident the Holy Spirit taught me mant things. One of the lessons I hold dearly in my heart from that incident is my realization that He knows me better than I know myself. Just like that sister did not know her own phone number but God did, I realized that He knows me more than I know myself. I have learnt to believe what He says about me to be true instead of trusting my own opinions of myself.

Another interesting thing I learnt that day is something I want to highlight in this chapter. In this incident, the Lord wasn't the source of this error(wrong phone number), her own memory was. But God's power is so mighty and His wisdom is so vast and His kingdom is so prevailing that He brought out a message for us in the midst of her weakness from this incident.

So that's my point. He can bring glorious things out of devil's cheapest strategies even though He is not the source of it. The moment you set your heart upon Him, there's a force released from heaven turning everything for your good, even the very weapons that were formed to destroy you.

Let me make my point clear, the Lord isn't dependent on the devil's weapons to do something glorious. That's not what I am saying. But I am saying, whatever the enemy plotted for your evil, God can turn it for your good. Sometimes even the very messes you had created for yourself without the knowledge of truth (demons exploit your ignorance), the moment you are in connection with Him starts turning in favour of you and His Kingdom.

In the coming chapters, I am hoping to bring better clarity on the same with biblical instances.

ROMANS 8:28 ALL AROUND THE BIBLE

CHAPTER ELEVEN

IN THE LIFE OF JOSEPH

We all know the story of Joseph. God gives Joseph a dream. God shows him the end in the very beginning because He is the Alpha and the Omega, the Beginning and the End.

Joseph shares the dream innocently with his father and brothers, and there begins the struggle.

Brothers are filled with jealously and they start plotting against Joseph.

Bible records jealously as a work of the flesh, motivated by demons.

So was this plot originated from God or the devil? Surely not God, but the devil. Do we find jealously in heaven? No! people are fully satisfied in the Lord. The works of the flesh such as jealousy etc have their origins in the fall of man with demons playing around it.

As we go through the story we understand God was on the move in the midst of all that the devil was doing against Joseph.

Own brothers throwing Joseph in a pit wouldn't have been a pleasant experience. It would have a definitely hurt Joseph... But God....

But God was with Joseph and the Bible says 'He was a prosperous Man' . When? When he was still a slave sold to the Egyptians, even without clothes.

> "*And the Lord was with Joseph, and he was a prosperous man; and he was in the house of his master the Egyptian.*
> *(Genesis 39:2,3)*"

And we see the devil trying to discourage Joseph over & over in different places and tries showing him, 'you are so distant from your dream', 'what God spoke to you isn't true' etc. But God was in the midst of it all. He was moving everything towards Joseph's destiny.

When Joseph was sold as a slave it looked nothing like he was moving towards the dream. Rather, it looked totally opposite. Then God prospered him where he was and he became second in command just next to Potiphar. Then for a while it looked like he was moving forward. Again when he was thrown into prison for refusing to sin, it looked like he again fell behind. If you notice, it would look like a fluctuating graph.

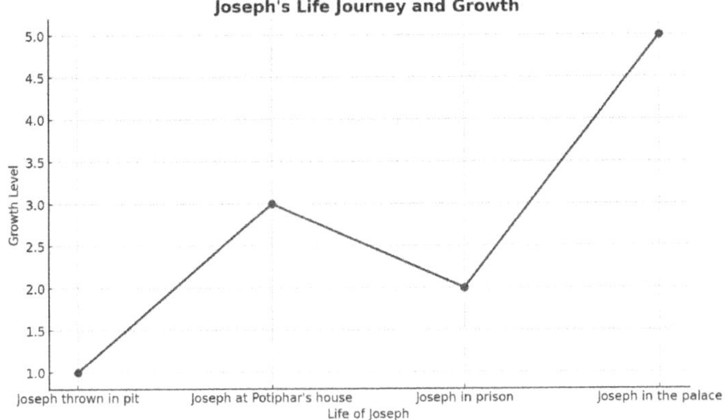

The life of Joseph to a human eye

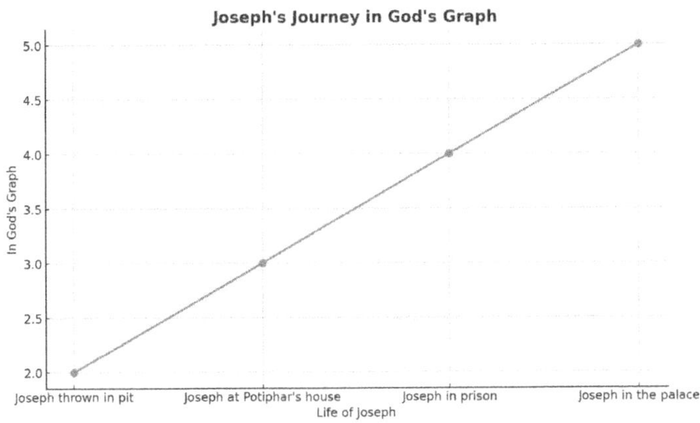

Joseph's journey in the eyes of God

But because God was with him, heaven's graph was never a fluctuating graph. He always made every plan/ attack of the enemy serve Joseph and put him on his path of victory. There was no setback according to God, because He was in the midst of it all.

As long as He is with you, your graph is never going to go backward, regardless of what situations tell you. It is all working together for your good to serve you.

If God's Word was not on Joseph's life, he could have toiled all those years and could have had a life that was less challenging but would have continued a normal life. But when God's Word is in someone's life, even when things appear like pulling you down, you and me are only getting propelled higher.

In case you are unaware if He is with you, here is the written proof to you:

"*Hebrews 13:5:*
"I will never leave you nor forsake you. "

Jesus came to us with the name, God is with us, "Emmanuel".

So if He is with you, which He is, your graph will always be upward and onward.

God's Partnership with one man makes a world of difference in person's life.

I wanna say that again:

"YOU WILL ALWAYS BE UPWARD AND ONWARD"

So let's get back to the story:

And finally when Joseph meets his bothers and the dream does come to pass, this is what, Joseph says.

"*Genesis 50:20*
But as for you, you meant evil against me; but
God meant it for good, in order to bring it about as

it is this day, to save many people alive. "

People's evil plans will only add an extra-ordinary favour, when the Lord God is with you.

49

CHAPTER TWELVE

IN THE BATTLE BETWEEN DAVID AND GOLIATH

One of the most impressive scenes in the bible is the scene of David and Goliath.

So let's get into the story.

"*1 Samuel 17:*

2 And Saul and the men of Israel were gathered together, and they encamped in the Valley of Elah, and drew up in battle array against the Philistines.

3 The Philistines stood on a mountain on one side, and Israel stood on a mountain on the other side, with a valley between them.

4 And a champion went out from the camp of the Philistines, named Goliath, from Gath, whose height was six cubits and a span.

5 He had a bronze helmet on his head, and he was [a]armed with a coat of mail, and the weight of the coat was five thousand shekels of bronze.

6 And he had bronze armor on his legs and a bronze javelin between his shoulders.

7 Now the staff of his spear was like a weaver's beam, and his iron spearhead weighed six hundred shekels; and a shield-bearer went before him.

8 Then he stood and cried out to the armies of Israel, and said to them, "Why have you come out to line up for battle? Am I not a Philistine, and you the servants of Saul? Choose a man for yourselves, and let him come down to me.

9 If he is able to fight with me and kill me, then we will be your servants. But if I prevail against him and kill him, then you shall be our servants and serve us."

10 And the Philistine said, "I defy the armies of Israel this day; give me a man, that we may fight together."

11 When Saul and all Israel heard these words of the Philistine, they were dismayed and greatly afraid.
"

Here Goliath challenges Israel and the army of Israel but no one from Israel had the guts to fight this giant Goliath except this little boy David.

He understood the power of God's hand that is able to deliver them from the hands of the giant.

Saul offers him the armor, but David denies the offer, and goes to war with his own weapon: 'a sling and five stones'. He knew, that it is not even those five stones that's is going to knock Goliath but God Himself.

Lets get more keen on this scene now.

"1 Samuel 17:

45 Then David said to the Philistine, "You come to me with a sword, with a spear, and with a javelin. But I come to you in the name of the Lord of hosts, the God of the armies of Israel, whom you have defied.

46 This day the Lord will deliver you into my hand, and I will strike you and take your head from you. And this day I will give the carcasses of the camp of the Philistines to the birds of the air and the wild beasts of the earth, that all the earth may know that there is a God in Israel.
"

Now wait! David says "I will take your head from you and give them as bread to the birds."

Wait! Wait! Wait! Didn't I read before that David denied all the weapons? So clearly he didn't have a sword or a knife.

Then how did he say he was going to take away Goliath's head? Where were his eyes? What was he looking at?

He was looking at Goliath's sword. David was so confident of God that, inspite of determining to cut off Goliath's head, didn't feel the need to carry a sword. He knew what was in the enemy's hand was sufficient. What an attitude! I so love that attitude. He must have imbibed it from our Father as he walked with Him.

1 Samuel 17:

"48 So it was, when the Philistine arose and came and drew near to meet David, that David hurried and ran toward the army to meet the Philistine.

49 Then David put his hand in his bag and took out a stone; and he slung it and struck the Philistine in his forehead, so that the stone sank into his forehead, and he fell on his face to the earth.

50 So David prevailed over the Philistine with a sling and a stone, and struck the Philistine and killed him. But there was no sword in the hand of David.

51 Therefore David ran and stood over the Philistine, took his sword and drew it out of its sheath and killed him, and cut off his head with it. "

GOD DID NOT NEED TO EQUIP DAVID WITH A SWORD.

GOD THOUGHT " HEY! GOLIATH'S SWORD IS SUFFICIENT"!

David and Golaith on the battle field

CHAPTER THIRTEEN

IN THE ARMY OF JEHOSHAPHAT

Let us also look into another incident from 2 Chronicles 20, Jehoshaphat leads the army...

> "2 Chronicles 20:12
>
> *O our God, will You not judge them? For we have no power against this great multitude that is coming against us; nor do we know what to do, but our eyes are upon You.*"

This verse shows they weren't armed enough.

> "2 Chronicles 20:15-17
>
> *And he said, "Listen, all you of Judah and you inhabitants of Jerusalem, and you, King Jehoshaphat! Thus says the Lord to you: 'Do not be afraid nor dismayed because of this great multitude, for the battle is not yours, but God's. Tomorrow go down against them. They will surely come up by the Ascent of Ziz, and you will find them at the end of*

the brook before the Wilderness of Jeruel. You will not need to fight in this battle. Position yourselves, stand still and see the salvation of the Lord, who is with you, O Judah and Jerusalem!' Do not fear or be dismayed; tomorrow go out against them, for the Lord is with you."
"

He bends down and worships the Lord and they start praising God.

He puts men in the front of the army only to praise the Lord and sing His praises.

"*2 Chronicles 20:21*

And when he had consulted with the people, he appointed those who should sing to the Lord, and who should praise the beauty of holiness, as they went out before the army and were saying:

"Praise the Lord,

For His mercy endures forever.""

And watch what happens next!

"*2 Chronicles 20:22-23*

Now when they began to sing and to praise, the Lord set ambushes against the people of Ammon, Moab, and Mount Seir, who had come against Judah; and they were defeated. For the people of Ammon and Moab stood up against the inhabitants of Mount Seir to utterly kill and destroy them. And when they had made an end of the inhabitants of Seir, they helped to destroy one another.
"

The Lord confused the enemy camp and they started fighting one another.

God didn't need to arm the army of Jehoshaphat. He turned the armies against one another. The very weapons of the enemies were enough for the Lord to deal with this fight.

When you know God and have a revelation of His true nature, the very weapons of the devil shall bow and turn around as weapons in the hands of God.

CHAPTER FOURTEEN

IN THE LIFE OF ESTHER

The book of Esther has a fantastic revelation of the Lord as the 'God of Romans 8:28'.

We see in the book, there are two key figures who stand opposed to each other. One is Haman, and the other is Mordecai.

Haman was instrumental in the hands of the devil to plot against the Jews and Mordecai was instrumental in the hand of God to save the Jews.

Because Mordecai refused to bow before Haman, Haman plots to kill Mordecai. As part of his plan, he even builds gallows in front of his house to hang Mordecai.

When the enemy was working at full force to destroy Mordecai's life, the Lord was working powerfully on the other side.

The King loses his sleep and starts reading the book of Chronicles and finds out that Mordecai had not been rewarded for what he had done for the King.

The King decides to honor Mordecai and asks Haman "what should be done to honor a man whom the King pleases?"

Haman assumed that it was about him and starts giving out a grand list of things he wished to recieve for himself. After the King hears them out, he asks Haman to do to Mordecai according to the list of things Haman had shared.

"*Esther 6*

1 That night the king could not sleep. So one was commanded to bring the book of the records of the chronicles; and they were read before the king.

2 And it was found written that Mordecai had told of Bigthana and Teresh, two of the king's eunuchs, the doorkeepers who had sought to lay hands on King Ahasuerus.

3 Then the king said, "What honor or dignity has been bestowed on Mordecai for this?"

And the king's servants who attended him said, "Nothing has been done for him."

4 So the king said, "Who is in the court?" Now Haman had just entered the outer court of the king's palace to suggest that the king hang Mordecai on the gallows that he had prepared for him.

5 The king's servants said to him, "Haman is there, standing in the court."

And the king said, "Let him come in."

6 So Haman came in, and the king asked him, "What shall be done for the man whom the king delights to honor?"

Now Haman thought in his heart, "Whom would the king delight to honor more than me?"

7 And Haman answered the king, "For the man whom the king delights to honor,

8 let a royal robe be brought which the king has worn, and a horse on which the king has ridden, which has a royal crest placed on its head.

9 Then let this robe and horse be delivered to the hand of one of the king's most noble princes, that he may array the man whom the king delights to honor. Then parade him on horseback through the city square, and proclaim before him: 'Thus shall it be done to the man whom the king delights to honor!' "

10 Then the king said to Haman, "Hurry, take the robe and the horse, as you have suggested, and do so for Mordecai the Jew who sits within the king's gate! Leave nothing undone of all that you have spoken."
"

And the story doesn't end there. Queen Esther tells the King that Haman was seeking to kill the Jews and her people. When the King entered, Haman was pleading before Esther for his life.The King found him falling on the couch, which he interpreted as assaulting her which added to the fury of the King.

"*Esther 7*

8 When the king returned from the palace garden to the place of the banquet of wine, Haman had fallen across the couch where Esther was. Then the king said, "Will he also assault the queen while I am in the house?"

As the word left the king's mouth, they covered Haman's face. 9 Now Harbonah, one of the eunuchs, said to the king, "Look! The [a]gallows, fifty cubits high, which Haman made for Mordecai, who spoke good on the king's behalf, is standing at the house of Haman."

Then the king said, "Hang him on it!"

10 So they hanged Haman on the gallows that he had prepared for Mordecai. Then the king's wrath subsided."

Then the King issues an order that Haman is to be hanged on the same gallows that he had made for Mordecai to be hung.

The hallow built

The Lord made a fool out of Mordecai's enemies.

The Lord worked so mightily that He rewarded Mordecai with the very hands of Haman and hanged Haman in the very gallows he had made for Mordecai to be hanged. Hallelujah! What a God we serve!

ROMANS 8:28 AND DEEP SECRETS OF SALVATION

The death of Jesus is something the devil thought He had the ultimate victory with.

But God used the devil's best shot against him and brought about glorious things.

I know the Lord has done so many things in this one death- the death of Jesus Christ.

In the coming chapters, I have shared few of the things I got to understand from my walk with the Holy Spirit.

CHAPTER FIFTEEN

JUDGEMENT OF THE RULER OF THE WORLD

John 16:7-10

"Nevertheless I tell you the truth. It is to your advantage that I go away; for if I do not go away, the Helper will not come to you; but if I depart, I will send Him to you.

8 And when He has come, He will convict the world of sin, and of righteousness, and of judgment:

9 of sin, because they do not believe in Me;

10 of righteousness, because I go to My Father and you see Me no more;

11 of judgment, **because the ruler of this world is judged.***"*

'Because the ruler of this world is judged'.

I have always marvelled at the wisdom of God and this revelation often reminds me that triumph always belongs to

Him regardless of how the situation looks like.

Have you ever thought, what it means when the bible says, 'now the ruler of the world is judged'?

The context talks about Jesus departing.

He says in John 16:7

> "*Nevertheless I tell you the truth. It is to your advantage that I go away; for if I do not go away, the Helper will not come to you; but if I depart, I will send Him to you.*
>
> *When He comes, He will reprove the world of sin, and of the righteousness and the Judgement.*"

So the context is this, that when Jesus will depart physically from the earth, the Holy Spirit will be given to us who will redefine our understanding of sin, righteousness and judgement.

So this is talking about the prince of the world, the devil being judged by the departure of Jesus. The departure of Jesus points to the death of Jesus on the cross here.

Now my question is, how was the devil judged by the death of Jesus? Why was he not judged before that?

To understand that, we need to understand the game the devil has been playing for ages.

It starts in the garden of Eden where Lucifer(devil) envies the unconditional authority given by God to mankind. He wanted to hurt mankind because he was jealous, but he had no power or authority to hurt them.

All dominion on earth was given to man who God made in His likeness and image.

The only way the devil could have his way in mankind is by man himself choosing to surrendering his will to the devil.

That's what happened in the garden of Eden. Man's nature got corrupted. His spirit which was so pure was polluted with sin. Now the devil started having his way from the inside of man through man's corrupted nature.

Now we all know this, 'The wages of the sin is death'. The devil wanted to kill, steal and destroy mankind. Through the sin nature in man, the devil had legal rights to kill any man. Death was something he desired to execute on every human and he happily kept executing it on mankind for thousands of years.

Hebrews 2:14

"Inasmuch then as the children have partaken of flesh and blood, He Himself likewise shared in the same, that through death He might destroy him who had the power of death, that is, the devil."

Let's say for example, there are some people who are put to death by the police department or army. Eg. terrorists, murderers, etc. Now even though they are put to death, we don't call it murder. Why? Because according to the law, it is due for them to die. Right?

The same way, when the devil was killing people before Jesus's arrival, because of the sin-nature in which they were born, he couldn't be charged guilty, because it was due for them according to the law.

But then, there comes a time, where a child is born of the seed of God Himself- Jesus!. There was no spot or blemish in him.

When Jesus came on earth and went around doing good, and healing all who were oppressed of the devil. , He became the devil's 'number one' headache.

Acts 10:38

""how God anointed Jesus of Nazareth with the Holy Spirit and with power, who went about doing good and healing all who were oppressed by the devil, for God was with Him"."

I can imagine, the entire force of demons all around the world gathering up and have group meetings plotting against one person-Jesus.

Right from his birth, he was trying and attempting to kill Jesus, but he just couldn't. Jesus just wouldn't die before He had to.

But these demons would constantly have their gang meetings plotting against the Son of God.

Now, coming back to John 16:11 "of judgment, because the ruler of this world is judged." And

John 12:31-33

"Now is the judgment of this world; now the ruler of this world will be cast out.

And I, if I am lifted up from the earth will draw all to myself.

This He said, signifying by what death He would die. "

Why is it that Jesus says, "Now is the judgment of this world; now the ruler of this world will be cast out"?

Considering John 16:11, The prince of the world was getting judged there.

According to these scriptures, when Jesus is lifted up is when the ruler of this world is getting judged.

John 12:33

This He said, signifying by what death He would die.

Verse 33 says it talks about the death of Jesus on the cross.

So in other words, the ruler of the world or I should say ex-ruler of the world was judged on the cross.

My question here is why on the cross and not before that?

The reason is because the devil had legal rights over every man/human being on earth until that day.

Man was born out of sin nature and according to the Word of God:

""The wages of sin is death" (Romans 6:23)"

So when he brought death upon people all through ages, he did it legally because of the laws of God already set in motion.

Man was bound to die because of the sin-nature inside of man.

Because this was legal for him, he wouldn't be judged.

If there was a court case against the devil "The wages of sin is death" is one legal claim he had to snatch away the lives of people on earth.

But when he touched the Son of God- Jesus Christ, he totally broke the law.

That's why the bible says,

"

1 Corinthians 2:8
"which none of the rulers of this age knew; for had they known, they would not have crucified the Lord of glory".
"

The devil just didn't know what he was getting himself into.

He thought killing Jesus would end his problem for a lifetime but the cross happened to marked the beginning of all his problems.

Since Jesus was sinless and spotless, it was illegal for the devil to touch Jesus' life. The moment he did it, immediately a judgement came from heaven upon the devil— "murderer!".

And upon the fall of this judgement over him, he was immediately cast out from his position "ruler of this world".

The devil no longer owns this position "ruler of the world" or "god of the world". He was the ex-ruler/ ex-god of the world".

And today Jesus says,

Matthew 28:18

> *"And Jesus came and spoke to them, saying, "All authority has been given to Me in heaven and on earth."*"

He is the Lord over this world today. He reigns over this earth today. And He has made us co-heirs with Him.

Romans 8:17

> *""and if children, then heirs—heirs of God and joint heirs with Christ, if indeed we suffer with Him, that we may also be glorified together."*"

A ruler is someone who executes his thoughts, his will and wants etc, in his domain of influence.

The devil used to carry out whatever he wanted.

But not anymore! Hallelujah!

Today Jesus reigns in and through us by imparting the knowledge of His will in us. Hallelujah!

CHAPTER SIXTEEN

THE LAMB AND THE HIGH PRIEST

Because of the way Jesus knew the Father, He was always oozing out Life.

As John 17:3 says "Knowing the Father is eternal life".

Life flows out of anyone who knows the Father. In addition, He was born of the very seed of God.

So striking Jesus with sickness wasn't something the demons could even dream of.

Watch this, Jesus said in John 14:30:

> *"For the prince of the world come, AND HATH NOTHING IN ME."*

He had nothing in Jesus, zero access in his body or soul or spirit. So he can't harm Him from inside. So he had no other option except trying to attack Him from outside.

So he plans to stir people against him, so that he could kill Jesus from outside through people who pay heed to his voice. And sadly, the bible scholars of the day couldn't discern the source of the voices they were hearing.

The religious – The Pharisees and Sadducees kept plotting against him under the inspiration of the demons.

Finally, the devil had an idea! 'Why not talk to high priest himself and get the job done sooner?'. He started planting grudge, hate and offense against the Son of God in the heart of the high priest.

Watch what happens here:

John 11:47-51.

"Then the chief priests and the Pharisees gathered a council and said, "What shall we do? For this Man works many signs. If we let Him alone like this, everyone will believe in Him, and the Romans will come and take away both our place and nation." And one of them, Caiaphas, being high priest that year, said to them, "You know nothing at all, nor do you consider that it is expedient for us that one man should die for the people, and not that the whole nation should perish." Now this he did not say on his own authority; but being high priest that year he prophesied that Jesus would die for the nation.
"

I am going to stop and ask you all a question right here.

If a person doesn't recognise Jesus as the Christ and plots so much evil against the Son of God in his heart, even to the point of putting Him to death, is it done by the inspiration of God or the devil?

Matthew 16:13-17.

"When Jesus came into the region of Caesarea Philippi, He asked His disciples, saying, "Who do men say that I, the Son of Man, am?" So they said,

"Some say John the Baptist, some Elijah, and others Jeremiah or one of the prophets." He said to them, "But who do you say that I am?" Simon Peter answered and said, "You are the Christ, the Son of the living God." Jesus answered and said to him, "Blessed are you, Simon Bar-Jonah, for flesh and blood has not revealed this to you, but My Father who is in heaven.
"

When Peter says 'Jesus is the Christ', he did not say it out of his human wisdom. There was God behind this scene. Flesh and blood did not reveal this to him but the heavenly Father Himself revealed it to him.

The same way, if a person cannot understand, and recognize Jesus as the Christ, it is not just a human lack of wisdom, there are active demonic forces behind their darkened understanding.

"2 Corinthians 4:4 (NKJV)
"In whom the god of this age has blinded the minds of unbelievers, lest the light of the gospel of the glory of Christ, who is the image of God, should shine on them."
"

After witnessing all the miracles Jesus performed, and with the sound knowledge of scriptures, it is not normal or mere humane for a high priest to want the death of Jesus. I believe, clearly there were active demonic forces involved in inspiring him to stand against Jesus.

Anyone who recognized He was of God, wouldn't be setting up and plotting against Jesus like this high priest.

According to what the Bible records for us in "John 11:47"

"Then the chief priests and the Pharisees gathered a council and said, "What shall we do? For this Man works many signs"."

Just to make it more stronger, lets look at what Jesus says here in John 8:42-44.

*"Jesus said to them, **"If God were your Father, you would love Me,** for I proceeded forth and came from God; nor have I come of Myself, but He sent Me. **Why do you not understand** My speech? Because you are not able to listen to My word. **You are of your father the devil,** and the desires of your father you want to do. He was a murderer from the beginning, and does not stand in the truth, because there is no truth in him. When he speaks a lie, he speaks from his own resources, for he is a liar and the father of it.*
"

So what's the point of knowing whether he was inspired of the devil or God?

Here's the point. As we already discussed and studied, there were demons plotting to kill Jesus using every opportunity they could.

The following is my imagination: but it is very possible that this could have happened in heaven at that time.

Angels telling the Father, 'Lord, these demons tried working with so many and finally got a hold of the high priest himself'.

And I see it this way, the Lord, who sits on His throne, with His majesty, completely undisturbed, completely unmoved.

The Lord would have said, 'Let him do it, I am just waiting for that'.

The devil thought that his master plan was a great success when the high priest agreed to the devil's suggestions and spoke forth: 'It is better for one to die'. He must have felt so proud of himself that day, believing it to be his smartest move of all.

But any time a sacrifice was offered to God in the Old testament, it had to be inspected by the high priest for blemish and it was the high priest who pronounced that the lamb is worthy to be sacrificed.

High Priest inspecting the lamb

Now the Lord had prepared Jesus as the Lamb of God for us to take away the sins of the whole world. The moment the high priest opened his mouth and said, "It is better for one man to die" pointing at Jesus, by law, Jesus became the perfect sacrifice pronounced by the high priest before God who would die for our sins once and forever.

That's why the Bible says it was a prophecy – it became a prophecy, fulfilling the plan of God.

> *"Now this he did not say on his own authority; but being high priest that year he prophesied that Jesus would die for the nation."*

It was as though the devil fell in his own trap.

God's wisdom is so huge that He can even turn the devil's greatest plans to play into His master plan. He is unbeatable and super abounding in wisdom. Hallelujah!

This is my personal opinion: I really felt many of the Psalms of David is just him sharing his heart to God in his pain. Surely God wasn't the cause of all those pains. I don't believe God allowed it as well. But God used those very same words to be prophecies for the greatest and only hope of the world – The Messiah .

Surely, He is a master redeemer.

He doesn't waste anything. He turns everything for your good.

CHAPTER SEVENTEEN

THE WHEAT CORN THAT DIES

John 12:24 NKJV

> "*Most assuredly, I say to you, unless a grain of wheat falls into the ground and dies, it remains alone; but if it dies, it produces much grain.*"

This is how the Kingdom functions. Have you seen a corn of wheat bearing fruit before it dies? We know, it never can.

But after it does die, do you see just one wheat coming out of it? Not at all. One died but many were raised.

Jesus was the corn of wheat that fell on the ground. The devil thought, his ultimate victory was in killing Jesus. He thought, if he crushed Jesus, God's prophecy would fail and that would be the end of 'her seed would crush his head'.

Genesis 3:15

> "*And I will put enmity*
> *Between you and the woman,*
> *And between your seed and her Seed;*

He shall bruise your head,
And you shall bruise His heel." "

Little did he know, he touched Jesus' life to bring about his own turmoil. The grain of wheat fell to the ground and there God rose many sons to glory right there.
Hebrews 2:10 NKJV

" "For it was fitting for Him, for whom are all things and by whom are all things, in bringing many sons to glory...." "

He became the first born of many brethren . All of his brethren were raised just like Him.
Romans 8:29 NKJV

" "For whom He foreknew, He also predestined to be conformed to the image of His Son, that He might be the firstborn among many brethren." "

The devil couldn't handle one Jesus on earth. Imagine what the devil has brought upon himself by killing Jesus on the cross, it is Jesus*millions. Millions of sons in the image and likeness of Jesus has been raised. Imagine his fate! Hallelujah!

Field of wheat harvest

CHAPTER EIGHTEEN

THE BRIDE WHO WAS HIDDEN

The death of Jesus has so many secrets hidden and we are only uncovering a few here in this book. The manifold wisdom of God has been deeply hidden in the death of Jesus on the cross and it accomplished redemption of mankind in so many different levels yet God hid it in the very the thing the devil thought he had his ultimate victory.

One such thing is the birth of the church. The church, as we all know, is the bride of Christ. Yet, where is she supposed to come from? Let's go to the beginning and see for ourselves.

Genesis 2:

> *"18 And the Lord God said, "It is not good that man should be alone; I will make him a helper comparable to him."*
>
> *19 Out of the ground the Lord God formed every beast of the field and every bird of the air, and brought them to Adam to see what he would call them. And whatever Adam called each living creature, that was its name.*

20 So Adam gave names to all cattle, to the birds of the air, and to every beast of the field. But for Adam there was not found a helper comparable to him.

21 And the Lord God caused a deep sleep to fall on Adam, and he slept; and He took one of his ribs, and closed up the flesh in its place.

22 Then the rib which the Lord God had taken from man He made into a woman, and He brought her to the man."

The woman was hidden in man. She came from man. So where was the bride of Christ, the church?

Right inside of Christ.

Watch this:

"Genesis 2:21–22 (NKJV)

21 And the Lord God caused a deep sleep to fall on Adam, and he slept; and He took one of his ribs, and closed up the flesh in its place.

22 Then the rib which the Lord God had taken from man He made into a woman, and He brought her to the man."

And this:

"John 19:32–35 (NKJV):

32 Then the soldiers came and broke the legs of the first and of the other who was crucified with Him.

33 But when they came to Jesus and saw that He was already dead, they did not break His legs.

34 But one of the soldiers pierced His side with

a spear, and immediately blood and water came out.

35 And he who has seen has testified, and his testimony is true; and he knows that he is telling the truth, so that you may believe. "

God opened up Adam's side, took a rib and there He made woman out of it.

So also, notice, Jesus' side was pierced open and there came His bride out of it.

Just like God caused a deep sleep to fall upon Adam and he took Eve out of him, He also caused a deep sleep to fall upon the Messaiah for three days. And when God wakes Him up from the sleep (raises Him from the dead), Lo and Behold, out of his side, the Lord birthed His bride: The church.

And now His bride will have her dominion on earth and the gates of hell shall not prevail against her. Hallelujah!

"*Ephesians 5:25–27 (NKJV):*

25 Husbands, love your wives, just as Christ also loved the church and gave Himself for her,
26 that He might sanctify and cleanse her with the washing of water by the word,
27 that He might present her to Himself a glorious church, not having spot or wrinkle or any such thing, but that she should be holy and without blemish.
"

The Glorious bride of Christ

CHAPTER NINETEEN

THE TESTAMENT AND THE TESTATOR

Hebrews 9:16-17 NKJV

"For where there is a testament, there must also of necessity be the death of the testator. For a testament is in force after men are dead, since it has no power at all while the testator lives."

It was just one death. But God made a million things move in just one death - the death of the Son of God.

God's Promises are God's will for us. Bible says "In Christ, all His promises are a Yes and Amen to us." (2 Cor 1:20). Why is it that it all gets unlocked only in Christ?

When the Bible says, in Christ, it always talks about our benefits of the death and resurrection of our Lord Jesus Christ.

Here is the reason why it all gets unlocked only in Christ and in His death:

The testament is in force only when the TESTATOR dies. At his death, begins the force of the testament. When Jesus died, immediately all of His promises began to come into force for His people. Hallelujah!

The testament

ROMANS 8:28 TODAY!

CHAPTER TWENTY

THE ART AND THE GREAT ARTIST

When I was working in a company in Pune, India, three of us girls used to share a house for stay.

I was blessed with fireballs in the Kingdom of God as my room-mates and they are very dear friends of mine till now.

One of the girl I stayed with is an artist and she used to paint some amazing paintings.

One day, as she was painting on the canvas right before me, suddenly by mistake her strokes went wrong.

For a minute I felt terrible that all her effort for the entire painting could become futile because of this one mistake.

When I asked her, she said, "Medo! For a good artist, there is nothing called a mistake. Any mistake becomes an art in the hands of a good artist". These words just stayed with me. She converted the very mistake into a beautiful art as she said.

Years later, when Lord started speaking to me on Romans 8:28, He told me "I AM A MASTER ARTIST" and I understood everything.

Initial picture

The Mistake

The Master artist- The Romans 8:28 God

Note: Link for the pictures(with color) is added (using QR code) in the end matter of the book in the section "Illustrative resources.

CHAPTER TWENTY-ONE

PAUL'S BOAST OF HIS WEAKNESSES

II Corinthians 12:9 NKJV

"And He said to me, "My grace is sufficient for you, for My strength is made perfect in weakness." Therefore most gladly I will rather boast in my infirmities, that the power of Christ may rest upon me."

Every one of us must have identified areas of our strengths and weaknesses. The areas we find ourselves strong are areas we rejoice about.

But look at Paul's philosophy (way of thinking). Paul says He will boast of his weaknesses. Why ?

He continues to explain: "so that the power of Christ may rest upon him". But why is that?

Why should the power of Christ rest upon him in his weaknesses? There is one thing that puts God off more than anything else- it is the 'self'. When a person is self-sufficient or to be accurate, they think 'they are self-sufficient', God cannot work with that person.

In reality, every one needs God: some know about it, some don't.

Paul here says that, he rejoices in his weaknesses, because that is the very place he is fully aware that he can do nothing about it and he is hopeless apart from His help from the Lord.

It is then God is able to have His full control and He is able to have His way. The power of God cannot rest in a place where 'self-strength' and 'self-dependance' is on the throne. But God's power rests in a place where 'self' is surrendered.

And our weaknesses highlight the presence of God in our lives like nothing else does.

Isaac may have sown many times and reaped many-fold. But what is recorded is when he sowed in famine and reaped a hundredfold. Famine was an area in which he was totally helpless . The source of the blessing/multiplication could not have come from anything he knew or understood. It has to be God and it was God.

Notice **the famine made the source of the multiplication obvious.**

So we rejoice in our weaknesses because it allows God to fully control those areas and it makes the source of our strength obvious to the world.

CHAPTER TWENTY-TWO

THE RIVER OF COMFORT

2 Corinthians 1

"3 Blessed be the God and Father of our Lord Jesus Christ, the Father of mercies and God of all comfort,

4 who comforts us in all our tribulation, that we may be able to comfort those who are in any trouble, with the comfort with which we ourselves are comforted by God."

There are areas where we may be deeply wounded and affected. May be it is a sickness, may be it is a relationship problem (God-ordained relationships), or may be it is a financial issue or sometimes just our own heart issues.

God is not the source of these issues. But according to these scriptures when we recieve the comfort of God in these areas, the comfort doesn't just solve our problems, but we become empowered to impart the same comfort to others because we have recieved grace.

We start carrying a river of comfort in the same area we had overcome. For an example, I used to be someone very fearful especially to face people. I could not look at someone face to face and talk. But God set me free from that fear, empowered me to preach His Word. Now, because I was weak in my flesh, in that area of my life, and I had to depend on God for His strength, God has empowered me to be a vessel who carries His strength in the same area for others. Glory to Jesus!

I rejoice because God has turned my areas of weaknesses to rivers of comfort for nations to drink of me.

CHAPTER TWENTY-THREE

WHERE SIN ABOUNDS, GRACE ABOUNDS MUCH MORE

This is one scripture which has confused me the most in the Bible. What does it mean when the scripture in Romans 5:20 says

> *"But where sin abounded, grace did much more abound,"*

Is God saying, it is good for a person to abound in sin so that grace could abound in him?

If we ask this question to ourselves "Is God promoting sin? Or will He promote sin?" We all would immediately scream a big NO! Then what does that scripture really mean?

The only way to rightly understand this scripture is through the right understanding of Romans 8:28.

Before getting into that, I feel we must first understand what Grace is.

One wonderful definition I recently heard: God's Riches At Christ's Expense.

Grace is God's unmerited favour. It is a divine empowerment of God over man where man fails in his own strength.

God's Grace is unlimited, uncontainable and indescribable. The riches of God's Grace would take an eternity to explore. I would like to try to help you a little here, to begin your journey of exploring the grace of God and His goodness.

The forgiveness we have in Christ is breathtaking. When I heard it first, I just couldn't believe what I was hearing. I was just thinking to myself "Could it be true?"

Colossians 2:13 NKJV

> *"And you, being dead in your trespasses and the uncircumcision of your flesh, He has made alive together with Him, having forgiven you all trespasses,"*

Well, that says, freely forgiven you all trespasses. Not some, but ALL. What does ALL mean? ALL includes our past, present and future sins.

Future sins? How can God forgive the sins I am yet to commit? It is because God is outside of time and He sees the end from the beginning. The sacrifice of Jesus is big enough to forgive all of the sins you have ever committed and will ever commit. Moreover, if you think about it, even all your past sins was future to the cross. If future sins can't be forgiven, even our past sins can't be forgiven.

So what does Paul mean when he says, "Where sin abounds, grace abounds much more"? Paul here explains the power of the redeeming hand of God. Sin was powerful to slay man in every possible way, but God's Grace has appeared to all men now through Jesus Christ. In the very areas where sin reigned over man, Grace now reigns and takes the upper hand, releasing the power of the Kingdom of God, in the very same areas, and enabling man to reign with Jesus.

Sin, which earlier served only to destroy man, now works to reveal the depth of God's grace to man. The deeper, 'sin' takes a man, Grace travels much more deeper for man's rescue, and sin serves to make someone realize how far God's love could travel to rescue and redeem him.

> "*Luke 7: 47 Therefore I say to you, her sins, which are many, are forgiven, for she loved much. But to whom little is forgiven, the same loves little.*"

God never wanted Adam to sin, but he did. But the Grace of God sent Jesus Christ, His only Son to die for the whole world. I wonder if man could have ever known,otherwise, that the Lord loved man to the point of death, that God would become man only to die on a cross and reveal His depth of love for mankind. God didn't make Adam sin, but Grace abounded much more when sin abounded, revealing the true riches of His grace: how deep, how wide and how far it is! Glory to Jesus!

BECAUSE GOD'S LOVE KNOWS NO END, THE DEPTH OF MAN'S SIN ONLY WORKED TO REVEAL THE DEPTH OF GOD'S LOVE.

CHAPTER TWENTY-FOUR

RESTORATION GOD'S WAY!

"So I will restore to you the years that the swarming locust has eaten..." (Joel 2:25 NKJV)

God is a restorer, and a redeemer, He can restore and redeem anything that was lost. It might be something you lost, through your own mistakes, but He is mighty enough to restore every bit of it. But the best part: God's way of restoration is always multi-fold.

Let's look at Job and His restoration.

Job 42:10 NKJV

*"And the Lord **restored** Job's losses when he prayed for his friends. Indeed the Lord gave Job **twice** as much as he had before."*

God restored Job mightily and His restoration was twice that of what he had lost.

"Proverbs 6:30-31 NKJV

People do not despise a thief If he steals to satisfy himself when he is starving. Yet when he is found, he must restore sevenfold; He may have to give up all the substance of his house."

God has set up laws for life on earth and He has also set up laws in His Kingdom. If a thief is found , God has demanded that the thief must restore seven-fold to the person he stole from.

John 10:10 makes it clear that it is the thief who comes to kill, steal and destroy. If you catch hold of the devil in any area of your life and you found him stealing from your life, it is time to demand your sevenfold back and it is rightfully yours. The King has ordained it so. It shall be restored to you sevenfold!

God's restoration is always multi-fold. So my dear people of God, expect the God of restoration to move mightily in the days forward in your life. God bless!

GOD STORY- EXPERIECING THE REDEEMING GENIUS

This story is so close to my heart. I thank God for allowing me to watch Him manifest Himself as a redeeming genius- The God of Romans 8:28.

There is a sister in the Lord known to me for quite some years . She was from a Muslim background. God touched her and mightily saved her from such a deep pit in her life. And rightfully, she was on fire for God.

But there came a time in her life where she had allowed the world to distract her from her first love- My Jesus. She fell in love with an unbeliever.

Now I am someone who is a very strong advocate of believers marrying only born again believers in the Lord. This is not my opinion but a clear instruction from the Word of God.

"2 Corinthians 6:14 (NKJV)
"Do not be unequally yoked together with unbelievers. For what fellowship has righteousness with lawlessness? And what communion has light with darkness?""

I tried telling her but the devil had blinded her so much that she couldn't see what we were cautioning her of, at that time. She went into that marriage and the marriage became a disaster. She really suffered through the marriage. She even came to a point that she wanted to divorce him.

She got back in touch with me once again and she was sharing her problems. I told her "Now that you are married, we cannot look back, we will have to believe God to turn this around".

I told her, "Yes! Whatever you did was completely wrong and was a total unwise decision. It is a decision totally contradicting the Word of God. We can never advocate anyone of marrying an unbeliever. Yet, God is a God who turns all things all for the good of those who love Him".

I gave her this scripture Romans 8:28 and told her that God is a master redeemer and a master artist. I prophesied over her that God would restore seven times to her. Even the very mistake she made God can turn it into a beautiful art. He can make it even better than before.

She returned to her first love.

She took that Word for herself and clung to it. She believed that God can turn her mistake into an art.

She stood her ground and walked with Jesus. The Lord began to move mightily in her heart and in her life. She began to bloom again. The Word of God transformed her mightily.

She started seeing changes in her husband. The very husband who was an agnostic (a staunch Hindu turned agnostic) once and had nothing to do with Jesus (matter of fact against Him), experienced the touch of Jesus right in his room. The encounter changed him and his direction forever.

Today he is a passionate born again believer who zealously wants to testify of what the Lord has done in his life. Now when we see the couple, it doesn't even look like there was a mistake in the middle, it has turned into a beautiful art in the hands of the Lord. Glory to Jesus!

I prophesy the same into your life right now: Your mistakes shall became an art in the hands of your Creator and the Lord shall restore sevenfold of everything you lost and YOU SHALL RECOVER ALL, in Jesus name! Amen.

To Know More About Us

Myself- Medona and my husband, we together lead Resurrection Glory International Ministries, based in Chennai, India. God brought about our union primarily for us to proclaim the message of "The Finished work of Jesus Christ".

Me and my husband

Check **rgim.co.in** to know more about us.

If you have been blessed by the book, write to us at **medona.shiphany@gmail.com** or text us at 7387515678.

Illustrative Resources

Check the following folder for illustrative resources:
https://tinyurl.com/yke98cex

or scan the below QR code:

Illustrative resources

Our Other Books

I have a small book available for any one wanting to recieve the gift of tongues.

The book is available on Amazon and Flipkart for you all to grab a copy. The book goes by the name "The Gift of tongues" by Medona Alfred.

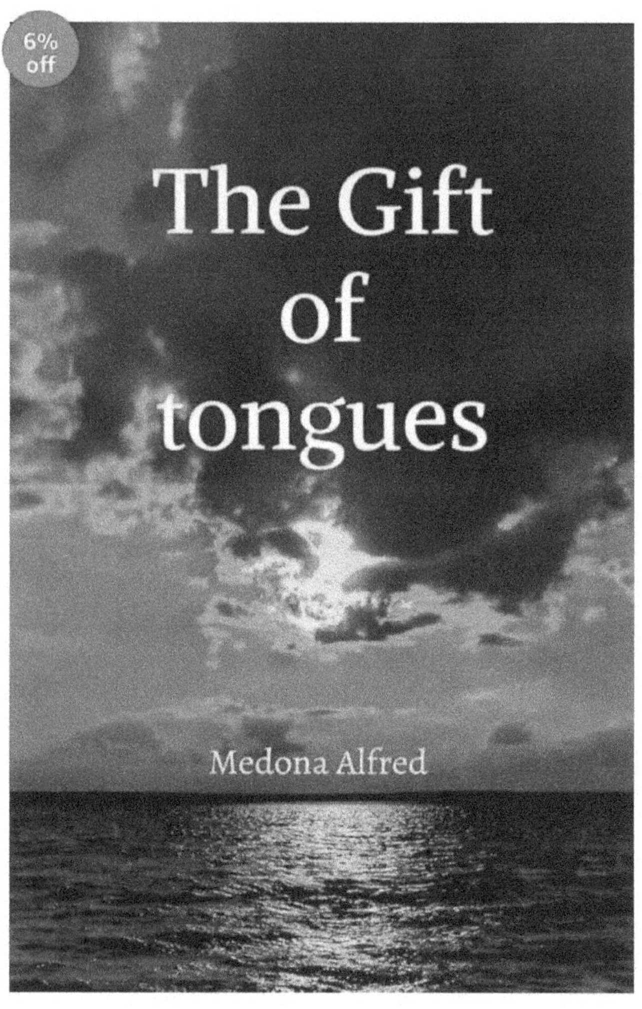

Cover page of the book "The Gift of tongues

I would also highly recommend reading another book written by my husband which expounds on God's promise of forgetting our shame, pain and hurts.

It goes by the name "Memory management- The blessing of forgetting" by Alfred Arputhakumar.

Memory
Management

The Blessing of forgetting

Alfred Arputhakumar

Cover page of the book "The Memory Management"